Entrepreneurship

MATTHEW G. KENNEY

ENTREPRENEURSHIP

MYTHS, REALITIES, AND REWARDS

2007

Entrepreneurship

ENTREPRENEURSHIP: MYTHS, REALITIES, AND REWARDS

Aspiring entrepreneurs often ask me "what is it like owning your own business?" My response is usually a boxing metaphor a very successful entrepreneur once shared with me: "If you're interested in the sport of boxing you can study the history, analyze techniques, and memorize statistics. But until you've been punched in the face you'll never know what it is like to be a boxer."

Entrepreneurship is very similar. Embarking upon an entrepreneurial career is a paradoxical experience. It can simultaneously be rewarding and terrifying. Taking the plunge may be easier if you remember that entrepreneurship isn't just about being self-employed, it's about being yourself. It is the pursuit of fulfilling your true potential, of simultaneously bettering your life, the lives of others, and managing your career on your terms.

Is your current career fulfilling you spiritually and professionally? If not, it may be time to strike out on your own. However, before launching a venture it's important to have a good understanding of the myths, realities, and rewards of an entrepreneurial career path.

This book is not intended to convince you to start or buy a business, rather the intent is to debunk the twenty most common myths I have encountered as both a business school professor and practicing entrepreneur. These myths, which are perpetuated at kitchen tables and in college classrooms, inevitably manifest into real-world misperceptions. Let's examine the twenty most common myths you will encounter on your entrepreneurial career path.

To My Parents, In Appreciation Of Their Unconditional Love And Support

MYTH # 1
80% Of Small Businesses Fail

While this myth is widely cited, the actual success rate of new ventures, according to recent research, is approximately 50%. About 28% of new ventures closed voluntarily and only 18% leave outstanding debt.

Mark Twain told us "facts are stubborn, but statistics are more pliable", and he was entirely correct. If we went to any business school across the country and asked the faculty "what percentage of new businesses fail?" I guarantee you the vast majority would answer "80%". But, the truth is that starting a business is simply not as risky as they are telling their students.

So then, is the failure rate for businesses 18% or 80%? My answer is...who cares? If you are thinking of starting a business why is the failure rate of other businesses really relevant? Scholars, pundits, and consultants love using statistics to prove their point. However, statistics pertaining to small business success and/or failure may not be valid or reliable because the majority of businesses in America are sole proprietorships and their closure rates are not closely tracked by the government.

What is more relevant is how you define the word failure. I truly believe that one of the biggest sources of conflict between entrepreneurs and non-entrepreneurs is that each group defines the word failure differently. To many members of society failure is viewed as the inability to accomplish a goal. To entrepreneurs, failure is defined as an *unwillingness to try and reach a goal*. Entrepreneurs focus on the process, not just the end result.

My entrepreneurial path illustrates this point. When I graduated from college I had a lot of ambition and eagerness to start a venture, I just didn't have any money. I was working in a family owned business as a deli manager and my father allowed me to develop some of our family recipes, which had been popular in our small town for years. Using a contract manufacturing strategy I outsourced the production and sold the finished goods to supermarkets and foodservice distributors throughout Massachusetts. This turned into a modestly profitable small business. However, there were some quality control problems so I decided to roll the profits into a fresh foods manufacturing business. Then a bigger problem occurred: I really didn't have the skill set needed to be a great manufacturer. I lost the money that was made from the first venture (and most of my savings), and by the age of twenty-eight was back at a square one.

I often tell my students that this venture cost me as much money as my college tuition but I learned much more about entrepreneurship from it than I ever did in college. First, it gave me a needed sense of humility. Losing money tends to remind us that nobody has all the answers. Secondly, it gave me a frame of reference as to the opportunities and risks associated with new product development, which I used to launch a consulting business.

My third venture, the aforementioned consulting business, focused on helping clients develop new retail products, establishing strategic plans, and developing food-safety plans. It was somewhat profitable, with hourly consulting fees as high as $125. Things were going well but then I did something most non-entrepreneurs can't fathom: I closed the venture voluntarily.

Why? I was offered a position to become Vice President of Operations of a private equity funded start-up and the opportunity was too good to pass-up. An optimist would look at my career path until this point and say that two of the three ventures were successful (33% failure rate). A statistician would see three business openings and three business closures (100% failure rate). As an entrepreneur, I view each venture as successful in their own way. In fact, for my personal, professional, and spiritual progression, the venture that lost money was actually the most beneficial.

So, Mark Twain was right. Statistics are pliable and we really shouldn't be unduly influenced by them. Do you think successful entrepreneurs really care about business failure statistics? Bankers may be influenced by this oft-cited 80% failure rate statistic, but aspiring entrepreneurs should not find it intimidating.

MYTH # 2
Entrepreneurs Are Risk Takers

Although this may be the societal view the vast majority of entrepreneurs do not view themselves as risk takers. Rather, they go to great lengths to identify and avoid risks. Successful business owners know that research separates ideas from opportunities. Therefore, entrepreneurs should be classified as *calculated risk takers*.

Is this just semantics? Not really. Launching a venture is more about mitigating risk than it is about taking risks. Just as Donald Trump wouldn't build a new hotel without knowing the projected costs and return-on-investment, you shouldn't start a venture without conducting a risk management analysis.

Opportunity recognition, not risk, is the cornerstone of entrepreneurship. However, this is often misunderstood by aspiring entrepreneurs. The word opportunity derives from the Latin word meaning *towards port*. Thus, you have to identify your personal and professional port of destination before you'll be able to analyze opportunities correctly. Look inward, find your passion and opportunities will manifest before your eyes. Once you recognize the best opportunity you can actually identify and avoid risks rather quickly.

Many times doing a simple feasibility analysis will help you decide if an idea is worth pursuing. Not every idea is an opportunity, so before you make the leap you really need to crunch the numbers. When I was serving as Entrepreneur-in-

Residence for Johnson & Wales University a student who had a novel idea for designing and making birdhouses approached me for advice. He was making them as a hobby and wanted to turn his hobby into a business. We were able to determine the potential feasibility of the venture by asking three questions:

Q. How much would you like to earn per year?

A. $60,000 (approximately $30 per hour)

Q. What is the retail value of each bird house?

A. $400

Q. How many hours does it take to make each birdhouse?

A. 20

Simple math shows us that his cost for labor would be $600 per unit ($30 x 20) while the revenue for each product is only $400. He has lost $200 and he hasn't even paid for materials yet. The venture simply isn't viable based on his original expectations. This simple exercise is really the premise for business planning. Most entrepreneurs do not like to write business plans as research can be tedious. However, research and planning are necessary to identify and mitigate risks. I know entrepreneurs who dismiss the importance of planning by stating that the plan will likely be useless because opportunities will exist tomorrow that can't be planned for today. There is some merit to this logic, but most consultants and scholars agree that the main benefit of writing a plan is to identify potential fatal flaws in a business model.

Planning doesn't guarantee success it just reduces the chances of going out of business. The best approach is to do a quick feasibility analysis. Nothing too deep, just look to see if the venture could make a profit using ballpark estimates. If the idea seems like it might be an opportunity, then produce a business plan to determine the profit potential.

MYTH #3
It Takes Money To Make Money

We have all heard the old saying *it takes money to make money*. But is this really true? How then do we explain successful entrepreneurs like Andrew Carnegie (U.S. Steel) or Howard Schultz (Starbuck's)? Each rose from poverty to become wealthy and successful. In reality, most ventures will require some start-up cash. The thing to remember is that it doesn't have to be *your* cash. There are many financing opportunities available to aspiring entrepreneurs. The secret to getting the money you need is to give potential investors the information they need to make an informed investing decision. After all, lenders lend and investors invest. If you have a plan to make them money it is in their benefit to help you.

Therein lay the secret to getting financed: give financiers what they need and they will give you what you need. Banks and private equity investors are willing and able to finance entrepreneurial ventures. Unfortunately, many aspiring small business owners don't prepare a comprehensive business plan that demonstrates the feasibility of their venture. If an entrepreneur is unable to project a Return-on-Investment for his/her financier it is unlikely he/she will receive financing.

Entrepreneurs usually have more options when it comes to financing their venture than they assume. The most traditional method is a Small Business Administration (SBA) 7a guaranteed loan. This is not a loan from the government, rather the government's way of assuring that banks lend to small businesses. The government insures 80% of the loan an SBA-approved bank gives you. Thus, if you default on the loan the bank gets the majority of their investment back. For example, if you default on a loan for $100,000 the SBA would give the lender $80,000. This mitigates the bank's risk but not your risk. You would be obligated to pay the government the balance of the debt if you default on the loan.

Lenders will usually require entrepreneurs to contribute 20% of the capital needs individually. If you are seeking an $100,000 loan you would be expected to contribute $20,000 of your own money in either cash or collateral. Bankers want to make sure you have a financial stake in the venture. They will also want you to have a good credit report for obvious reasons. If your business plan calls for purchasing real estate your lender would likely point you toward the SBA 504 loan program, which finances real estate purchases. The investment required for entrepreneurs participating in this program can be as little as 10% of the total loan request.

If you don't have any money to invest and/or you don't want to assume the risk of paying back loans your best option would be to seek equity financing. You generally won't have to pay an investor back if the venture fails, but the trade-off is that you will be giving up a percentage of ownership in the business.

Some ventures may be conducive to a business model called contract manufacturing (this model has been used successfully by fashion designers and other brand-oriented product marketers for years) whereby production and distribution are outsourced. Once a prototype is developed the entrepreneur can pitch the product to buyers; receive a purchase order; and borrow against the purchase order using a financing strategy called *factoring*.

Contract manufacturing is a great strategy for young companies that don't have the money or inclination to build a production facility. In 2000, I joined a start-up baked goods venture called Jessica's Wonders as Vice President of Operations. Within eleven months the company, led by a very talented entrepreneur named Jessica Nam-Kim, was selling products in over 300 supermarkets throughout New England. Yet, we didn't own a single delivery truck or bake a single cake ourselves. Rather, we identified strategic alliances to produce and distribute the products according to Jessica's specifications.

My first business utilized this business model as well. Starting with nothing but some great recipes and hard work I was able to have my products distributed by SYSCO, one of the country's largest distributors. Just remember that there are many ways to get the money you need if you are dedicated, passionate, and creative. It will take some money for working capital to make your dreams a reality but if other people can find the resources to launch a business so can you.

The key thing to remember is that if you give investors what they want (a strong plan with a projected return on their investment) they will give you the financing you need.

MYTH # 4
The Customer Is Always Right

The old adage "the customer is always right" is a wonderful sentiment but not entirely true. In reality customers may drag you into fragmentation, act unethically, and treat your employees disrespectfully. A better adage is *"the customer always has rights"*, such as the right to receive your best effort and exceptional customer service.

Anyone reading this book with even a modicum of work experience will probably agree with me when I say *the customer isn't always right.* That doesn't mean, however, we should take an adversarial position toward customers or disagree with the positive sentiment upon which the myth is based. The benefits of focusing on customer service are well documented. Companies with high customer service rankings out perform their competitors and enjoy a good return on Customer Relationship Management (CRM) investments. The problem, as I see it, is that some customers actually believe that they have the inalienable right to disrespect a company's employees if they believe it is in their commercial interests.

If you ever want a great illustration of this myth watch the television show Airline®, which airs on the A&E Network and chronicles Southwest Airlines employees interacting with customers at several terminals across the country. You'll likely see passengers who get drunk while waiting for their flight and then become abusive when they are prevented from boarding.

Or, you may see a passenger getting in trouble for passing himself off as a sky marshal etc. You get the idea. It makes for great television, but every time I watch the program it is validation of my decision to exit retail years ago.

Don't get me wrong, every company and entrepreneur is going to make mistakes that lead to frustrated customers. And there are times when the customer is right. If a customer's complaint is valid then, as an entrepreneur, you need to find the root of the problem and fix it. We just can't be intimidated by customers, especially when we know their complaints are not warranted.

Perhaps the biggest risk of believing that the customer is always right is that it leads entrepreneurs to side with their customers reflexively rather than first getting insight into the problem from his/her employee(s). Most entrepreneurs will tell you that it is easier to find a new customer than it is to find and keep a good employee. Therefore, we should strongly consider the human resource management ramifications before assuaging consumer demands.

The adage that the customer is always right is rooted in sound logic. My advice, which again cannot be stressed enough, is simply to adjust the adage to state *the customer always has rights*. They have the right to expect your best effort and consistent professional service. They just don't have the right to denigrate your employees or demand you modify your processes to meet their needs.

MYTH # 5
Good Employees Are Hard To Find

One of my most gratifying experiences as a professor occurred during my first year of teaching. I bumped into a student who was giving her mother a tour of the campus and we had a nice discussion about all of the things the student had learned and how much she enjoyed college. Then the student turned to her mother and said: "Professor Kenney started our first class by saying: you'll hear people say good employees are hard to find. Don't believe them, good employees are everywhere. The problem isn't with the employees it is with the leaders."

I was very impressed that she remembered this and asked if she remembered what I suggested she say to herself every time that she heard someone make this statement. Without missing a beat she said "you can make money or excuses...you can't make both." Her mother and I were so proud.

As managers, we need to keep in mind that problems with employees are like weeds. To permanently remove a weed we need to remove the root. Yet, often managers don't take the time to identify the root of the problems they are dealing with. If they did they would see that the company's culture and/or processes are usually the root of the problem.

Let's debunk this myth first by defining the term *management*. Management is the process of accomplishing organizational objectives through planning; organizing;

staffing; leading; and controlling. The word management is derived from the Latin word for hand, so it's helpful to look at the five functions of management (planning, staffing etc.) working similarly to the way five fingers of a hand work together. Each finger has a distinct role but when they work in unison they are capable of truly amazing things.

If you find yourself in a work situation where a manager has bought into the myth that good employees are hard to find consider if the manager and/or company is creating an environment where the five functions of management are working in unison. If the five functions of management are not working in unison problems will inevitably occur.

For example, back in the late 1990's I was retained as a consultant by a small but rapidly growing restaurant chain. A kitchen manager from their largest facility was complaining one day about how *good workers are hard to find*. It seemed like all of his problems would be solved if he could just find good employees.

One day I asked if we could grab a cup of coffee as I had a few questions for him relating to the problems he was having with employees. As a young consultant I was cognizant that it was important that I didn't come across as the smarty-pants / know-it all type. In fact, the reason I knew this manager was the root of the problem was because I made the same mistakes when I was managing employees in my family business. However, through experience I learned that the best way to educate someone is to allow them to come to his/her own conclusions. The transcript of our conversation would have looked something like this:

Question: *Who is responsible for hiring employees?*
Manager: *I am.*

Question: *Who is responsible for training the employees?*

Manager: *I am.*

Question: *Who is responsible for leading and motivating the employees?*

Manager: *I am.*

Question: *Who is responsible for the high turnover and poor performance?*

Manager: The employees.

I could see on the manager's face that he was beginning to recognize his culpability in the problem when I asked him to ponder, not answer, the following questions:

- Do you have a pool of qualified candidates that you can draw from?
- Do you have an orientation / training program?
- Are the goals of the company clearly articulated to the employee?
- Do you know the hopes, dreams and aspirations of employees?

These questions were rhetorical, of course, since we both knew that the answer to each question was "no". To answer "yes" to each of the aforementioned questions the manager would just need to make a few inexpensive modifications to his operational processes. We'll examine each question individually:

How do you develop a pool of qualified candidates?

The genesis of the process can be found in your business plan. If the sales estimates projected in your financial plan are accurate you should be able to project your human resource needs up to 12 months in advance, which gives you time to find the right person for the job. Just keep in mind that there must be congruence between the goals of the company and the goals of the employee. If there isn't it is unlikely that the employee will be committed or productive.

There are reasons why big companies get bigger and small companies tend to struggle. One of the reasons is that bigger companies are more proactive in seeking the talent they need. When seeking talented people it is best to go to places where talented people congregate to pursue their chosen avocations, primarily schools offering some sort of vocational training. For instance, some of the most successful food service establishments in America work closely with Johnson & Wales University to gain access to aspiring chefs, hoteliers, and managers. This is a win/win situation as the employers are guaranteed a steady stream of talent, and students often gain assurances of full-time employment before graduating. 98% of Johnson & Wales graduates attain full-time employment within six months of graduation.

When seeking hourly or part-time workers high schools and trade schools can also be a rich source of prospective employees. My family relied on a steady stream of high-school students to work in our delicatessen and catering business for years. All you need to do is contact the career / guidance counselors at your local high school and let them know what qualities you are seeking. You can also post advertisements online and network (offering existing employees rewards for recommending qualified applicants is a strategy used by a college I teach for), the idea is to just be proactive. You can't be proactive, however, if you don't know your projected employment needs. Remember the words of Benjamin Franklin "by failing to prepare, you are preparing to fail".

Do you have an employee orientation / training program?

In all honesty most small business owners would answer "no" to this question. However, designing a training program isn't a costly proposition. It simply requires a commitment to educating new employees as to the policies and procedures of the company. Every company has policies and procedures, most just don't put them in writing. Using off-the-shelf software, any company can print up an employee handbook, which should include:

- The company's Mission Statement
- The company's goals and objectives
- An organizational chart
- A diversity statement
- Clearly stated expectations
- Opportunities for advancement
- Explanation of benefits

It is also important to assign each employee a mentor. This will benefit the protégé but also empowers the mentor. A company that does these simple things will see a dramatic decrease in their employee turnover and vastly improved productivity.

Are the goals of the company clearly articulated to the employee?

A better question for managers might be does your company have clearly articulated goals? The number of small businesses operating without a business plan has been estimated as high as 70%. Is this estimate too high? As with all small business data you have to be a bit skeptical. At some intellectual level every small business owner has a plan in his /her mind. After all, this is not a career path for the myopic. Most entrepreneurs have a vision of where they would like to lead their company. Even those who plan to remain at status quo have a plan. It is not ambitious, but it's a plan.

The problem is that many entrepreneurs don't write their plan down on paper. Ken Proudfoot, founder of the Rhode Island Youth Entrepreneurship Program and 2006 National Recipient for the Leavey Award for Excellence in Private Enterprise Education once told me "if it is not written, it is not real." Truer words have never been spoken. Unless a manager is fortunate enough to employ a psychic the chances of miscommunication and misperceptions arising grow exponentially when plans are not in writing.

This process should actually start before you hire an employee. Begin by sharing your mission statement, which is simply a brief statement describing the organizations reason for being. For example, Microsoft's mission statement is: *At Microsoft we work to help people and businesses throughout the world realize their full potential. This is our mission. Everything we do reflects this mission and the values that make it possible.*

Note that the mission statement doesn't lock the company into a particular path but it sets a tone that is forward looking and ambitious. If you want to work for Microsoft you better be forward looking and ambitious too, since it doesn't seem like the type of work environment where people can just punch a clock and go through the motions.

Once the company's mission is shared with a prospective employee it is then imperative that the manager share with him/her the responsibilities of the job. This *job description* lets the employee know exactly what will be expected of him/her. If at this point there seems to be congruence between the mission of the company and the goals of the employee both parties can move forward. If not then both parties can go their separate ways. Managers will find the right employees if they take a scientific approach to human resource issues and it all starts by getting the company's goals down on paper.

Do you know the hopes, dreams and aspirations of your employees?

Have you ever noticed that many big companies discuss

how well they treat their employees? This assuages their guilt, in my opinion, for treating job prospects like dirt. I doubt there is any worker who has gone through the job hunting processes without being curtly dismissed or ignored all together. Human resource recruiters generally don't have a marketing background, so maybe they don't see the damage being dismissive has on a company's goodwill. Maybe they just don't care. They've got the money and provide the benefits employees need so they call the shots. There is nothing prospects can do about it. Right?

Wrong. Disenchanted corporate sector employees are a blessing for small business owners. We may not be able to give them more money or the best vacation packages but we can give them a sense of dignity. Organizational behavior research shows that sociological and psychological factors tend to be more important considerations to employees than salary. Therefore, small business owners are well positioned to tap the vein of employee resentment that pulsates within Corporate America and draw talented people into their organization.

When interviewing candidates it is best to focus on the needs of the applicant rather than the needs of the company. This is something that many managers don't comprehend but it is essential for hiring success. The small business manager already knows his/her goals, what he/she doesn't know are the hopes, dreams, and aspirations of the applicant. My advice would be to start the interview by asking the applicant "of all the things you can do with your time and talent, why do you want to work here?"

They'll think to themselves: "this manager recognizes I have talent." How may corporate interviews start-off with a positive vibe like that? Unfortunately, sometimes you won't get a good response because the answer requires a little bit of thought. One method I have used in the past is to mention to the applicant how the word career is derived from the Latin word for *vehicle,* thus their career should be a vehicle to take them from where they are to where they want to be. I ask "three years from now where would you like to be both personally, and professionally? How can this opportunity get you there?"

If the applicant's aspirations are not in alignment with the company's mission it will be immediately apparent to both parties. The applicant might not be right for the job but they will be appreciative of the fact that you care about them and hopefully you will have played a valuable role in helping the applicant on the path toward his/her true vocation. As an entrepreneur never under estimate the profoundly positive impact you have on the people you meet. 43% of the U.S. workers, according to a Gallup poll, dream of owning their own business. They dream of being like you, don't disappoint them.

MYTH # 6
Health Insurance Is Cost Prohibitive

According to the U.S. Small Business Administration's Office of Advocacy the issue that is of greatest concern to small business owners is the cost and availability of health insurance. Possibly you've seen news reports about escalating costs of health care and wondered how you would afford the same level of benefits if you left your job and pursued an entrepreneurial path. If you have that is an indication that you are a prudent decision maker.

Only 52% of firms with fewer than ten employees offer health insurance to their employees. By contrast, 99% of firms with over 200 employees offer health insurance to their workers. Thus, it is clear that bigger businesses have a real competitive advantage when it comes to attracting qualified candidates. I'd prefer to work for a company that offered benefits, wouldn't you? To add insult to injury large companies actually pay less per premium than small businesses owners due to an economic principle known as *Economies of Scale.* Essentially, the more they spend the more leverage they have to negotiate better rates.

So, how is it possible for an entrepreneur to lower his/her health care premiums to the same level as big businesses without sacrificing quality? The answer lay in the same economic principle. Of the twenty-five million businesses in America, 99.7% are classified as small businesses. By joining together small businesses can negotiate health insurance premiums equal to, or lower than, those negotiated by large companies.

In many states associations have been formed to serve this purpose. For example, the Massachusetts Business Association helped me secure a health insurance premium from the nation's top ranked health plan for about $300 per month. This is less money per month than what my employer was paying for my health care premium in 2000 without a decrease in the level of quality.

Nobody likes paying $3,600 per year for health insurance but this expense certainly isn't cost prohibitive. It is a tax-deductible cost of doing business that is calculated into the entrepreneur's budget. If the entrepreneur has a spouse and/or children then the monthly premium he/she could expect to pay would likely be in the $750—$1,000 per month range. This amount can be a little more intimidating, especially when there are no money coming in yet, but if the company can't generate enough cash-flow to pay $12,000 per year in health care premiums we need to go back to the business plan and determine if the venture is really viable.

Another option for small business owners who want to lower their monthly premium would be to purchase a High Deductible Health Plan (HDHP). With this approach, a percentage of your income is set aside tax-free in a Health Savings Account (HSA). If you incur incidental health related expenses the money is drawn from the HSA. However, if you need hospitalization or face a catastrophic illness your health plan would be activated after you paid the higher deductible. The maximum out-of pocket expenses vary depending on whether your policy is for an individual or family.

One of the biggest dilemmas facing small business owners is whether or not to provide health insurance for employees. It really comes down to a simple philosophical question: should we view health benefits as an expense or an investment? Historically small businesses have viewed them as an expense while large companies have viewed them as investments.

If you hope to grow your business my advice would be to view the act of providing employees benefits as an investment. Paying $300—$1,000 per month/per employee requires a lot of commitment but the decision to invest isn't purely altruistic. You will receive a positive Return-on-Investment, including a reduction in employee turnover. For example, the average cost of recruiting and training an employee is over $13,000 so minimizing employee turnover has a dramatic impact on a company's bottom line.

Dr. Abraham Maslow offered a theory suggesting that human beings have a hierarchy of needs. The theory being that basic needs, like safety, need to be satisfied before people can satisfy higher-level social, self-esteem, and self-actualization needs. This theory has its advocates and protagonists within the academic community, but it seems obvious that employers who satisfy an employee's basic need for security by providing fair wages and health benefits are more likely to attract and retain qualified employees. This isn't really rocket science, it should be common sense. Unfortunately many small business owners only see the money going out and don't see the long term tangible and intangible benefits of providing health benefits.

To prove *Maslow's Hierarchy of Needs* theory ask yourself if you would accept a full-time job offer if it didn't include health benefits. Will you be able to attract qualified applicants who have a spouse and/or children without including health benefits as part of their employment package? I doubt it. Why should they incur risk needlessly?

The bottom line is that we should treat employees the way we would want to be treated. One way to satisfy an employee's need for safety, thereby increasing the likelihood they will become motivated to get the most of their talents, is to *invest* in health benefits. Doing so is not cost prohibitive rather it will pay a positive return-on-investment in the form of increased employees commitment and productivity.

If your company isn't generating enough cash-flow to pay for health insurance then you need to go back and analyze your business plan and daily operations. Identify where revenue can be generated and where expenses can be minimized but be careful not to cut health insurance investments without considering the resulting negative ripple effect it will have on your human resources. Neglecting to provide full-time employees with health care benefits is tantamount to telling them you don't care about their most basic needs.

Providing health care for part-time employees is a bit trickier. Some companies, like Starbuck's, offer benefits to employees who work a minimum of 20 hours per week. This would likely be too cost prohibitive for the average entrepreneur. However, you may want to consider consolidating several part-time positions into one full-time position or matching employee contributions to their Health Savings Account.

MYTH #7
You'll Have To Sacrifice Time With Your Family

The average work week for entrepreneurs is 52 hours, while the average work week for American workers, according to the Bureau of Labor Statistics, is just under 34 hours. As these statistics suggest you can expect to spend more time working as a small business owner, but you can also find time for friends, family, and social activities. The origin of this myth is tied to the fact that many small business owners spend much more than 50 hours per week running their business. Therefore, non-entrepreneurs assume that excessive hours are a pre-requisite to success. What these people don't understand is that entrepreneurs often *want* to spend more time in their ventures. These small business owners are doing what they love, which is why they are spending so much time at work.

An entrepreneurial venture is a little like a romantic relationship. When you are in the process of falling in love with a person you don't really view a lot of time spent with that person as excessive. You spend time with the other person because you want to. The emotions awakened in a start-up are obviously not romantic, but they are real and powerful. When pursuing a venture that you view as your vocation and a culmination of your dreams it is easy to lose track of time. This isn't always healthy for your interpersonal relationships, but most experienced entrepreneurs will tell you it is a reality.

There are, in fact, many entrepreneurs who are devoting more hours to their business than they would prefer. However, this is usually a reflection of poor planning, inadequate working capital and/or ineffective leadership.

Before launching a venture it is essential to have a plan that identifies your working capital and human resource needs. Simply put: how much money and how many people will you need to get the business up and running? If you don't secure enough cash you will be playing catch-up from day-one. You will be forced to spend a disproportionately large amount of time performing day-to-day operational tasks instead of looking at the big picture leadership issues.

It is my contention that learning to balance leadership responsibilities and management responsibilities is the most difficult aspect of entrepreneurship. However, if you can learn to perform this delicate balancing act you will be well on your way to having a profitable venture that affords you ample time for family and social endeavors.

In a traditional corporate setting there are three distinct levels of management:

Executive Level: the responsibility at this level is to set long-term goals and assure that the company's mission is being fulfilled. Executives are strategic thinkers who understand how the principles of management, marketing, and finance interact.

Middle Management: this level focuses primarily on implementing the strategy you have set and training your staff to achieve organizational objectives.

Entry Level: this is the lowest level of management but is vitally important because it relates to the day-to-day operational tasks that need to be done.

In a corporate setting the responsibilities of each level are well established and there will be a clear chain-of-command expressed in the form of an organizational chart. In a start-up venture the entrepreneur is usually, at least initially, responsible for performing the tasks of all three levels simultaneously. Some entrepreneurs, including myself, like this aspect of entrepreneurship. When operating my manufacturing business there were days where I would make a sales presentation to a multi-billion dollar retailer then drive back to the production facility and peel potatoes so we could get a shipment of potato salad out the door. This role ambiguity isn't appealing to everyone but it does assure against your day being boring.

Every entrepreneur should perform leadership (big picture) and management (day-to-day operations) activities. The challenge is striking the right balance. Focusing too much on the big picture ideas will result in poor operational efficiencies. Focusing too much on performing operational tasks yourself will result in missed opportunities and organizational stagnation. One needs to look no further than the myriad of venture capital financed start-ups of the late 1990's for examples. Many of the companies that failed had great ideas but tried to get too big too quickly.

The entrepreneurs who launched many of these failed ventures were brilliant technicians, but wanted to be great leaders without also being effective managers. On the flip side, many small businesses stagnate because the entrepreneur is a good manager but can't lead effectively. Small businesses often stay small because the entrepreneur is hesitant or unable to take the venture to the next level. If a company is not moving forward it is really moving backwards since competitors will continuously be targeting its customer base and offering new product or service offerings.

MYTH #8
Entrepreneurship = Self-Employment

Richard Cantillon, an Irish economist studying in France, is widely credited with coining the term entrepreneur in 1734, although there is evidence that the term had been used sporadically prior to his landmark *Essay on the Nature of Commerce in General*. To Cantillon, an entrepreneur was an individual who recognized an opportunity and coordinated resources to pursue it. He felt that one needed to be self-employed to be an entrepreneur.

The view within the academic community that entrepreneurship is synonymous with self-employment prevailed until the early 1930's when economist Joseph Schumpeter declared that entrepreneurship is not contingent upon self-employment. Entrepreneurship is, in the Schumpeterian view, dependent upon the qualities employees possess and whether they create value for the firm. From this belief emerged the philosophy of corporate entrepreneurship, which is also known as intrapreneurship. Although Cantillon would have viewed corporate entrepreneurship as being oxymoronic most academicians today agree that entrepreneurs should be viewed as those possessing the following traits: creativity, autonomy, flexibility, and a willingness to be a moderate risk taker.

Following this interpretation self-employment would be deemed a manifestation rather than a condition of entrepreneurship. The literal translation of the combined

French prefix and suffix for the term entrepreneur is *between takers*. One party should take money and the other party should take goods and/or services in return. This is a simple concept for 21st Century readers but was a radical thought in the early Eighteenth Century. Remember, capitalism hadn't yet been invented. In fact, Cantillon is one of the few authors cited by Adam Smith, whose 1776 publication *The Wealth of Nations,* positively influenced America's Founding Fathers.

Corporate entrepreneurship is one of the fastest growing areas of academic research because it has been shown that companies that embrace entrepreneurhip principles are likely to out perform their competitors. Many successful companies have recognized that entrepreneurially inclined employees can be valuable contributors to a company's success if their skills are nurtured. Converting employees with entrepreneurial aptitude into corporate entrepreneurs can deliver exceptional value to stakeholders. Companies like 3M have thrived due to strategies that embrace corporate entrepreneurship principles. Numerous successful products, including the Speed Pass®, were the direct result of corporate entrepreneurship.

Most companies don't have a corporate culture conducive to entrepreneurship and inhibit entrepreneurial employees by implementing policies and procedures that stifle the aforementioned entrepreneurial traits. As a result, entrepreneurial employees leave the organizations and pursue their own ventures. However, these entrepreneurs may be better off finding a company that has a culture complementary to their entrepreneurial skills rather than launching a new venture.

Let's say that you have recognized in yourself some entrepreneurial aptitude but you don't want to launch a venture by yourself. What should you do? My advice would be to identify a company that has an entrepreneurial orientation, as this will scratch your entrepreneurial itch, and provide you with the structure and/or security you are seeking.

There are five dimensions of entrepreneurial orientation which you should look for in potential employers if you are considering corporate entrepreneurship as a career path: autonomy, innovativeness, being proactive, competitive aggressiveness, and risk taking.

Corporate entrepreneurship ventures can be initiated either internally or externally. However, the most common scenario involves an aspiring entrepreneur seeing an opportunity in the market and attempting to obtain company resources to pursue it. While entrepreneurially oriented companies will facilitate opportunity recognition and pursuance they will also impose internal barriers that challenge aspiring corporate entrepreneurs. Before deciding to take this path you also need to look inward and understand your entrepreneurial personality. Serial entrepreneurs may be less likely to succeed in a corporate environment compared to an entrepreneur who has considerable corporate experience. The differences between corporate cultures and small business cultures are vast and complex.

If you currently work for a company and would like to use their resources to launch a spin-off venture you may find it comforting to learn that your thoughts are in alignment with most successful corporate entrepreneurs. There is something to be said for not reinventing the wheel. If your company has an entrepreneurial orientation it may make sense to become a corporate entrepreneur. Intrapreneurship isn't for everyone, but it is a career path worth considering.

The following transcript is from an interview conducted with Kenneth Proudfoot, an experienced entrepreneur and educator, for an article I co-wrote for The *Journal of Applied Management and Entrepreneurship* entitled Understanding Corporate Entrepreneurship: A practitioner perspective of organizational intrapreneurship. Mr. Proudfoot's perspective on this subject provides great insight into what entrepreneurs can expect if they pursue corporate entrepreneurship. The venture he is discussing is an entrepreneurship center he conceived and implemented for a large university:

Question # 1: What do you feel is the biggest challenge facing corporate entrepreneurs?

The biggest challenge facing corporate entrepreneurs is the corporate culture itself. The corporation is a hard setting for entrepreneurs to create, although it is an inviting setting in which to create because there are so many undiscovered and untapped opportunities lurking in every corporation.

Question # 2: Did your company have an organizational commitment to foster corporate entrepreneurship?

The university originally had an entrepreneurial culture, but it was pushed aside as the suits took over the business. Re-creating it was fun. And the original stakeholder thought it was cool and supported us. Unfortunately, the suits won and crushed the effort.

Question # 3: Was your motivation to initiate this venture intrinsic, or influenced more by external factors?

The adventure we embarked on was totally internally generated, brought about by seeing the need and seeing the opportunity in the organization, that is, there was a vacuum. The students were there, but there was no support facility. It seemed obvious to me to propose an entrepreneurship center.

Question # 4: What is the biggest benefit of launching a corporate entrepreneurial venture?

The biggest benefit was seeing the reaction of the students and also being able to provide a physical place for outside entrepreneurs to come in and work on their projects and also be mentors to our college students.

Question #5: What role can Corporate Entrepreneurship play in retaining high performing, committed employees?

Corporate entrepreneurship is a great tool for retaining entrepreneurial employees who want to deviate from the corporate program and develop new ideas, new business models, and new products. Just making such opportunities available will attract and hold committed employees.

Question # 6: What role, based on your experience, should training play in Corporate Entrepreneurship development?

Training, learning, whatever you want to call it should be promoted, especially if it is training in something new, different or revolutionary (that is, different) from the normal path of the existing employee (i.e., send corporate scientist to training program for aeronautics (flying). Shake her/him up!

Question #7: Would HR selection tests be helpful in identifying potential corporate entrepreneurs?

Not familiar with such tests, but doubt any sort of test can identify the characteristics that come out naturally as a person works in a business. That person will self-identify.

Question #8: In an organizational behavior context, what are the risks associated with Intrapreneurship?

Corporate entrepreneurship shakes up the status quo. It makes people crazy. It makes non-creative bosses insecure. It makes others in the organization, if person has successes, very jealous and angry and motivates them to interfere and undercut the entrepreneur's activities.

Question #9: Do you think it is better to keep new ventures in-house, or set them up separate from the influences of the parent company?

New ventures should be set up in-house. Some determination should be made later to decide if the activity or business should become part of the business, be moved outside the firm's normal operations to another location or site, be sold to another company, or sold to the creators.

Question #10: What lessons did you learn from this venture that you will apply to your next corporate entrepreneurship venture?

Do not try to change a non-entrepreneurial corporation into an entrepreneur-loving business, especially when founders have moved on and only bureaucrats are minding the shop. Pursue new ideas below the radar. Also, if you need the corporation's money, research, and/or patents to succeed with your idea, bring the project fully formed with financing/funds attached before ingratiating oneself to a partnering corporation.

***

If you are contemplating bringing a new business idea to an employer remember that any idea you have at work generally belongs to your employer, not you. Therefore, if you have an idea for something that is patentable, or has significant commercial potential, discuss the idea with your personal attorney first. Remember, ideas are assets and assets have value. Determine the value of your idea, and protect it if possible (trademark, patent, copyright etc.) before you share it with anyone.

MYTH # 9
Family Businesses Lead To Family Problems

Have you ever felt misunderstood? For example, have you ever shared your perspective with someone and they look at you like you are from another planet? This is how I feel just about every time I discuss family business dynamics and business succession statistics with business school professors. Academicians love to use data to show causal relationships. However, many times the data does not reflect the truth. Yet they continue to cite meaningless statistics because, many times, that's all they have. Most have never worked in a family business so they don't have a clue about what they are talking about. Professors look at data that says only 30% of family businesses are passed from the first to second generation; and that only 15% are transferred from the second to third generation and this tells them that there are all sorts of organizational problems.

Many researchers fall into the same trap of thinking that a low succession rate somehow correlates to dysfunctional family dynamics or failure, when often the opposite it is true. This actually may be a sign of a healthy family. In all fairness to well meaning professors and researchers, unless they have grown-up in a family business this may not be obvious.

For example, do you expect your children to one day live in your house? Your house, like your business, is just an asset. Most parents would want their kids to go out and live their lives on their terms. They don't have to stay in the town they grew-up in, attend the same colleges as their parents etc. Yet, when it comes to family businesses there seems to be this ridiculous perception amongst professors, some management practitioners, and others within society that businesses that do not progress from one generation to the next are somehow failures.

In our society a banker would not presume that her child will become a banker. Why then would we assume that the child of an entrepreneur would become an entrepreneur? If the child is an entrepreneur the chances are, from my experience, that they will use the family business as a springboard rather than a security blanket and go off and do their own thing. To me, that's success.

This last point really cannot be emphasized enough. Entrepreneurs who grew-up in a family business setting are likely to define success differently. Consider their perspective: they were raised in an environment where one or both of their parents were creating value and doing their own thing on a daily basis. Some may have been fortunate to learn at the knee of entrepreneurial grandparents as well. Through observation and osmosis these children were gaining first hand knowledge about what an entrepreneurial career path is really all about. Their perspective on employment is not better than those who were raised in a more conventional environment, but it is very different.

Some children of entrepreneurs may look at an entrepreneurial path replete with rewards and sacrifices and say thanks, but no thanks. Others may share the passion of their parent(s) and join the family firm, while others are inspired to go out on their own. When you think about it, why would professors and so-called small business experts expect there to be a high succession rate for family businesses? Especially when we assume that the succeeding generation will have access to more money, opportunity and education than the previous generation.

Let me share an actual example of a family business that in my mind symbolizes the American dream and illustrates the true spirit of a family business. On March 1st 1933, the week President Roosevelt closed the nation's banks symbolizing the height of the Great Depression, a 28 year old entrepreneur nick-named Sonny opened a small grocery store. Through hard-work and exceptional customer service he was able to carve a niche in a small New England town and raise a family. As Sonny's children grew so did his business and he was able to eventually send his children to better schools than he had attended and eventually his youngest son, Paul, joined the business after graduating from college.

Paul shared his father's work ethic and reputation for exceptional customer service. He, like his dad, was a true gentleman merchant. However, Paul also saw the big picture and began diversifying the company into more profitable areas. Rather than buying perishable foods and simply re-selling them the company began developing its own recipes and soon had the most highly regarded delicatessen in the area. After earning his MBA, Paul expanded the company by building a 100-seat restaurant adjacent to the original location of the family store as well as building a catering division. In fact, Paul was recognized nationally by his peers in the catering industry as a pioneer and expert in the field of corporate catering.

As the family business grew so did Paul's family. He had six children, all of whom spent time working for the family business throughout their youth. However, only Paul's youngest son pursued the family business as a career. That youngest son, as you may have guessed, was me. Working with my grandfather as a child, and more closely with my father as an adolescent and adult had a profoundly positive effect on my life and career. Perhaps the greatest gift my father gave me while working together was the gift of freedom. He did not pressure me to join the family business, even though as the youngest child and the one who took the most interest in the business I was the presumed heir who would carry on the company tradition. Actually, my father encouraged me to go work for someone else after graduating college but I was eager to join him and grow the venture.

I began to realize, however, that I did not share my grandfather's passion for retail or my father's skill and passion for the catering business. I had some modest successes, like selling products to supermarkets and large distributors but my passion was in educating others. So, upon my father's retirement in 1996 I moved on to other ventures and we closed the family business after 63 years of continuous operation.

While not continuing the family business was the most difficult decision I have ever made, replete with guilt and numerous moments of self-doubt while I followed my own path, looking back I am confident that I made the right choice. Business school professors may view me as a failure or a statistic, but who cares? The truth is that successful family businesses cannot be measured by statistics, only by the love, closeness and the mutual respect family member maintain for each other. Businesses come and go, but a family's love is forever.

Of course, there is no shortage of dysfunctional family businesses out there. However, the myth that family businesses lead to family dysfunction is easily debunked. It is likely the other way around, dysfunctional family relationships lead to dysfunctional family businesses.

MYTH # 10
Franchises Are Much Less Risky

One of the most common myths propagated by proponents of franchising is that 90% of franchises are successful. This is a case of people using semantics to separate you from your money. Franchisors, such as McDonald's and Subway, do in fact have a strong record of success. After all, many are well established business concepts with a long track record of profitability. However, many franchisees who purchase the rights to run individual businesses are not nearly as successful. Research I've seen suggests that about 38% of franchised units ultimately fail. This closure rate is statistically less than the rate of non-franchised venture closings, as discussed earlier, but when you consider the high cost of entering a franchise a case can be made that they are riskier than traditional start-ups.

This is not to say that that franchising is a bad option, only that the risk of going out of business is not dramatically less. For example, in 2002 New England residents were ecstatic about the news that Krispy Kreme was coming to town. So called savvy entrepreneurs were plunking down millions for the right to sell these deep fried delights to waiting hoards of consumers. Krispy Kreme, it was reasoned, had a superior product to New England's own Dunkin Donuts, which is one of the most successful franchise concepts ever. Therefore, there was no downside.

When Krispy Kreme arrived in the area it looked like it was going to be a huge success. People were (I kid you not) literally camping-out in front of the franchises to be the first to get these sugary sensations. I'm not sure if this is a good example of the power of branding or a better example of America's obsession with junk food. But it is true, store openings were media events and everyone it seemed needed Krispy Kreme donuts. The entrepreneurs were proven right, or were they?

A few years later the franchisees were out of business and the parent company was in a state of fiscal crisis. The millions of hard earned dollars poured into these franchises disappeared as quickly as those first donuts that rolled of their greasy conveyor belts. What went wrong? Franchisees bought into the myth that franchises are less risky and thought nothing could go wrong. A wise man once told me "there is dough in donuts", which may be true when marketed correctly but that doesn't mean that one should invest their savings in a donut franchise without doing adequate research.

If these entrepreneurs had done their homework they would have seen that Dunkin Donuts is not a donut company they are a coffee company. 63% of their revenue comes from beverages, like coffee, which people generally consume daily. Krispy Kreme, by contrast, was a fad. It was delicious fad but a fad none the less. And, if there is one immutable law of franchising it is don't invest in fads.

MYTH #11
Working From Home Is The Answer

Ask anyone who runs a home-based business what they like most about working from home and you'll inevitably get a response like "I love the freedom" and "my commute takes less than a minute." Without a doubt there are some great benefits. But many of the aspiring entrepreneurs who I have counseled in seminars and classrooms throughout the years seem to believe that working from home is the answer to all of their problems. A magical panacea for the problems associated with *going to work* for a living. In further discussions with home-based entrepreneurs, if they are honest, you will likely glean that working from home can be professionally limiting and lonely.

In 1911 Fredrick Taylor wrote *The Principles of Scientific Management*. An engineer by training, Taylor realized that employee productivity could be increased if some of the variables associated were changed. For example, slightly increasing the size of a shovel could increase the amount of coal dispensed into a furnace without increasing the amount of labor. Productivity, therefore, could be increased by scientifically studying and measuring employee actions. The *science of management* was born.

In the early 1920's a researcher by the name of Elton Mayo wanted to build on Taylor's theory so he went to the Hawthorn, Illinois facility of Western Electric Company and studied employee behavior. His hypothesis was that employee behavior would increase or decrease depending on physical variables, such as light and temperature. So, the studies began. Mayo and his team turned up the lights the employees increased their productivity. They turned down the lights and employee productivity increased some more. They turned down the heat and productivity increased. They turned up the heat and productivity increased. No matter what physical variable they changed employee productivity increased. This defied all logic, what was the cause?

What Mayo and his team found was that employee productivity was not influenced by physical variables as they had predicted, but rather by the fact that employees were being watched by Mayo and his team. Supervision played a much greater role in employee behavior than the actual work environment.

Aspiring home-based business owners assume that their new work environment will enhance their productivity, which isn't too logical considering their proximity to their family, television and/or comfortable bed. More importantly what they neglect to consider is that their productivity is going to be impacted more by a lack of supervision than it is by the actual work environment. Of course, you may be thinking "entrepreneurs are self-starters so they do not need supervision to the same extent employees do", which is true provided the aspiring home-based business owner *is* an entrepreneur.

Just as buying a piano doesn't make someone a musician starting your own business does not make you an entrepreneur. Starting a business makes you a small business owner not necessarily an entrepreneur. There is a big difference between the two. Most entrepreneurs show signs of thinking differently very early in their life. They may be drawn to a family business, have a paper route, sell lemonade etc. Most have had some sort of entrepreneurial experience before running a full-time home based business. They have certain talents in networking, or identifying opportunities that make them good candidates for a home based business. Their comfort with ambiguity will see them through tough times.

Home based business owners that do not possess these entrepreneurial traits may find it difficult to become properly motivated without some sort of supervision. It is easy to complain about managers, but sometimes they push employees because they need to be pushed. I am not the patron saint of corporate managers and in reality I think a majority of them have no idea how to manage or lead employees, but they are not all wrong. Some employees need the structure and supervision managers provide even if they resent it. An aspiring home based business owner really needs to be honest in determining if he/she can live without the security that Corporate America provides.

When comparing the perks of a home office to a corporate office he/she may also want to do a skills inventory to see how many of the required business skills he/she possesses. Entrepreneurs by nature and experience tend to have an eclectic skill set. A good entrepreneur will have a general understanding of marketing, management and accounting but will primarily focus on identifying and seizing opportunities.

By contrast larger businesses have people in place to perform certain functions. Accountants monitor accounts; salespeople sell; managers manager etc. Aspiring business owners sometimes neglect to consider that just because they are good at their particular trade does not translate to having functional competencies in other areas of business. You can be the greatest salesperson in the world but if you can't manage your business you are in big trouble. Home business owners who neglect this fact will soon find themselves back in Corporate America with a lot less money in their pocket.

A home office is one place where it pays more to be a generalist rather than a specialist. Of course, some of this risk can be mitigated by outsourcing certain functions and focusing on your core competencies but home based businesses are essentially micro-enterprises by design. You are going to have to develop competencies for things you do not enjoy and that may be, in all honesty, minutia.

Spending time on minutia leads to a serious problem for home-based business owners: opportunity costs. Every minute you spend doing a task that is beneath your skill level you are not maximizing your earning potential. For example, if you earn $90/hr as a graphic artist but spend 10 hours per week doing administrative work this work has an opportunity cost of $900 ($90 x 10). Wouldn't it make sense to hire an assistant for $400 per week to do administrative tasks for you? Doing so saves you $500 per week. Unfortunately, because opportunity costs do not involve an actual cash outlay many small business owners ignore them. The law of comparative advantage says if someone can do it cheaper you should outsource the function to them. This is a good economic principle to remember.

Another consideration often overlooked when launching a home-based business is loneliness. Take if from someone who has worked from home for years…it can be a very lonely career path. Let me share an example, the most common measure of job satisfaction in America is the Job Descriptive Index (JDI), which was developed by researchers from Bowling Green State University in 1969. It is generally considered to be one of the most statistically reliable and valid scales available to both practitioners and academicians. When these two groups agree on something you know it must be good.

The JDI measures five dimensions of job satisfaction: work performed; pay; opportunity; supervision and co-workers. Two of the five most important facets of job satisfaction (supervision and co-workers) relate directly to interaction with fellow employees, while opportunity for promotion is also heavily influenced by co-workers and organizational dynamics. Supervision and co-workers are dimensions of this scale because research on job satisfaction dating back to the 1920's shows that interaction between co-workers and managers greatly impacts satisfaction. If these elements are essential for job satisfaction, how is the small business owner who has neither supervision nor co-workers going to remain satisfied?

Some home-based business owners will likely derive enough satisfaction from their work and pay to mitigate the impact of not having supervisors or co-workers. Also, having a strong social network can alleviate some of the loneliness. However, you get the idea. Working with others is essential to achieve satisfaction and if you lose that by working from home you may find that working in an office isn't as bad as you once thought.

Personally, I do not recommend working from home if it can be avoided. The money you spend on office space may be a good investment as it provides structure, normality, and credibility to your venture. I always thought working from home would be great but to me it has been a case of something not being as good as it seems. If you like people, you need to go out and meet them.

MYTH # 12
Having A Great Product Or Service Is The Most Important Ingredient Of Success

Are you reading this book because you have a great product or service that you want to sell? Are you certain that it could be successful if you could just get people to try it? Having a great product or service is a start but it does not ensure success. To prove this point let me share a story from my own entrepreneurial career.

My family delicatessen was famous in our local community for having some great fresh foods. In particular, we had a potato salad that was very popular. We would steam potatoes with their skins on to retain their flavor and hand peel each while very hot. We would then mix in the ingredients and the resulting product was superior. I know everyone likes their recipe the best, but this really was a great product. One day my father and I were talking to a customer who happened to be a supermarket executive. When he learned I was beginning to sell products wholesale he put me in-touch with the chain's deli buyer. By the end of the week we were selling our potato salad in three local supermarkets. Within a couple of months we were selling to more than twenty stores across eastern Massachusetts.

At the time I was very excited about the company's future because the potato salad brands we were competing against were so bad, from my perspective, they were almost inedible.

Made by the ton and loaded with preservatives the products tasted like they should be sold in the pet food aisle. Yet, I no longer make food products at all and my former competitors are still selling the same wallpaper paste, I mean, potato salad. How could this be? Not only was my product better it was vastly outselling the competitors up until the day I closed shop. What went wrong?

I forgot that having a great product doesn't always matter. The marketing mix, often called the 4 P's of marketing, consists of production, pricing, placement (distribution), and promotion. The companies that manage their marketing mix the best will succeed regardless of the quality of their product. Think about it, are there any retail products you have bought that were absolutely terrible? Why did you buy them? Your decision was probably influenced by price, the point of purchase, or an advertisement. If you have low pricing, good distribution and effective promotions people will likely buy, at least once, what you're selling.

The main problem I faced with my potato salad venture was that the product could not be mass distributed profitably. In order to really grow the business I needed to distribute the product via the chain's central distribution facility. Unfortunately, the distribution channel was not designed to handle highly perishable products like mine (product wasn't being rotated etc.). Thus, I would have needed to add preservatives, which I refused to do, so I chalked it up as a lesson learned and moved on to my next venture.

I hated the supermarket industry so I was happy to leave. However, I cost myself a lot of time and aggravation by not having done a marketing plan. If I had done one I would have seen the potential distribution threats and invested my resources elsewhere. If you have a good marketing plan you are well on your way to establishing a successful brand. You're not there yet, you still need to master some of the intangible elements such as positioning, target marketing, and customer service, but your foundation is strong.

When looking at the production facet of your marketing mix define the word quality correctly. Often marketers fall into the trap, as I did in my younger days, of fixating on the "my product is better than yours" view of quality. This is a subjective view and should be avoided. Rather, look at quality as a Total Quality Management (TQM) or Six Sigma practitioner would. They view quality as setting and reaching pre-set standards. That's it. A competitor may set lower quality standards but that means they are probably charging a lower price and are targeting a different market. For instance, the competitors I mentioned earlier were selling potato salad for $1.19 per pound. My product was selling for $2.99 per pound. In theory we were competitors but we really were not selling to the same target markets. Their quality was appropriate for their target market, not mine.

Entrepreneurs that sell higher quality products often get frustrated because their product is obviously the best option for customers. Sure it "costs a little more", they say but if customers would just try it once they would be hooked. If you think this way too I understand, I once thought this way as well. Then I learned another immutable law of marketing: some people are just cheap.

If your product costs a nickel more than the competitor's they don't want it. Do you know people like this? Don't they drive you insane? I don't mean people who are somewhat frugal, which is actually an admirable trait. Seeing Wal-Mart founder Sam Walton, then the world's wealthiest man, driving around in an old pick-up truck was actually kind of cool. However, people that are penny wise and pound foolish are simply not worthy of your promotional efforts. You can't build a brand catering to these cheapskate consumers unless you are a low-cost provider, like Wal-Mart, which precludes most small business owners.

MYTH #13
Big Companies Are Your Biggest Threat

Previously I mentioned how I was able to sell products to a large supermarket chain. My company also sold to other larger retailers and foodservice distributors, including SYSCO, the nation's largest foodservice company. Later on I did some consulting for several large companies and came to an interesting conclusion: large companies offer many more opportunities for entrepreneurs than they do risks. Don't look at your largest competitors as threats, rather an opportunity to carve your niche.

Growing up as the youngest child in a large family one learns not to pick a fight you cannot win. I'm not sure why it took so long for me to learn this as an entrepreneur but hopefully you won't make the mistakes I made. If you are in an industry that has an 800 pound gorilla, let's say a small retailer competing against Wal-Mart, you may find that you need to focus solely on your core competencies and become a niche player to compete. If this happens you will reap the financial rewards. There truly are riches in niches.

Every time a competitor treats one of their customers rudely, or takes customers for granted, they are doing entrepreneurs a huge favor. We just need to be aware of what's going on and position our companies as better *service* providers. Customer service is the Achilles heel of many big businesses. They have mastered the marketing mix but many still treat customers like numbers on a balance sheet and this represents a huge opportunity for entrepreneurs.

Economic theory and history tells us that large companies are always going to have cost advantages over small businesses. For example, a small soda manufacturer is not going to pay the same price per pound for ingredients as Coca-Cola. In fact, the prices won't even be close. Economically there is no way that a small competitor can match Coke's low product cost. They may be able to sell at the same price point if they cut their profit margin and don't advertise. But even then it is doubtful they could match Coca-Cola's price point. So what should they do? Savvy entrepreneurs know that competition is a wonderful thing as it validates an opportunity and allows them to search for unfilled niches. The aforementioned soda maker should let Coke and Pepsi kill each other in the mass market and focus on more lucrative niche markets. For example, they could develop creative packaging and target younger audiences, urban markets, health conscious consumers, ethnic specialty sodas etc.

Many entrepreneurs are surprised to learn that many large companies, including retailers, have programs in place to assist small businesses become vendors. Stop & Shop, New England's largest supermarket chain actively promotes a diversity program that includes expanding their vendor base to include more small businesses, especially women and minority owned ventures. Companies that collect large government contracts are often required to share the wealth with small business vendors, and high-tech companies, such as Microsoft, actively invest in start-up ventures.

The reason why Fortune 500 companies and other large firms encourage partnerships with small businesses is not altruistic, it is good business. They know what their weaknesses are and small businesses help them mitigate two of the biggest: 1) being disconnected from the local community and 2) stimulating new ideas and opportunities.

When I was selling to large retailers I learned that many store managers were empowered to purchase locally produced products based on the logic that it creates goodwill in the community. The product has to reach quality and profitability standards set by higher level executives but if it does entrepreneurs will have their products on store shelves in short order. In the supermarket industry it is not uncommon for buyers to have open buying sessions a few times per month where entrepreneurs can come in and pitch their products. Getting products on store shelves really isn't as difficult as many entrepreneurs assume they just need to do a little more homework.

The biggest reason for investing in start-ups is that some large companies know that the 'next big thing' could be worth billions. Generally you only see companies investing in entrepreneurial ventures if the start-up has some sort of technology patent. A patent gives a company the sole rights to market an invention for twenty years. Entrepreneurs who have a patentable idea need to speak with a patent attorney before pitching their idea to anyone. But once their rights have been legally protected, they will find there is shortage of potential investors and/or strategic partners if the patent has upside potential.

The key thing to remember is that big companies are big for a reason...they are very good at what they do. However, they also tend to be poorly perceived by communities; are in need of a more diverse vendor base; and need innovative ideas. These weaknesses offer a wealth of opportunities for entrepreneurs if we can resist the temptation to view large companies as competitors.

MYTH #14
Anyone Can Become A Successful Entrepreneur

The title of this section may sound strange to readers since the author is an entrepreneurship professor. One would think that I and other professors in this subject area get paid to make people entrepreneurs. Yet, this is not really what we do. Good professors simply teach students how to refine their talents and become better entrepreneurs. Creating entrepreneurs is God's domain. Professors can't teach people to be entrepreneurs, only help those with God given entrepreneurial talent refine their gifts.

To illustrate this point with my students I like to use a baseball metaphor. I ask them: "how do you hit a curveball?" An interesting discussion usually arises and a lot of advice comes forward such as hire a hitting coach; research the pitcher; consider the count; steal signs from the catcher etc. All of these are good suggestions, but the fact remains that the batter needs to have the natural talent to get a hit. Practice, in this case, does not make perfect. Practice, in combination with natural talent makes perfect.

Nova Southeastern University's School of Business and Entrepreneurship is named for Mr. H. Wayne Huizenga, who holds the distinction of being the only entrepreneur in history to lead three Fortune 500 companies. When students study Mr. Huizenga's accomplishments they are inspired and glean valuable advice but professors cannot teach students to be like

Mr. Huizenga because his personality and gifts are unique unto himself.

If you have ever been to the Musée du Louvre in Paris you know how humbling and inspiring it is to be in the presence of great artwork. The feeling you receive is difficult to explain but the sense that these great artists, such as Leonardo da Vinci, have a God given talent is overpowering. No art teacher would ever claim that they can teach a student to be like Leonardo, Picasso, or Michelangelo. Instructors can help students appreciate art and refine latent artistic ability, but they cannot teach people to be artists. Artists are born, not made.

Professors and consultants who think entrepreneurship can be taught like the sciences of management, marketing and finance forget that entrepreneurship is an *art*, not a science. Just like Leonardo, who turned a blank canvas into the Mona Lisa, entrepreneurs are in the business of turning intangible ideas into tangible assets. Entrepreneurs and artists both create things of value by combining their talent with limited resources. Michelangelo carved David from a discarded piece of marble. Harlan Sanders started Kentucky Fried Chicken, at 65 years old, with nothing but a recipe. Isn't the end result that both men created something of enduring value? Do you think that any professor can teach a student to accomplish what Michelangelo or Colonel Sanders accomplished? Can this type of creativity be taught? I don't think so.

I have shared my view that entrepreneurs should be considered artists with many people over the years. Entrepreneurs tend to embrace the metaphor quickly, while artists tend to hate it. The idea of someone comparing beautiful art with commerce repulses them. I recall a student at the Rhode Island School of Design getting very upset when I compared what I do to what she does. After she was done calling me a capitalist pig for saying that business is as beautiful and important as art I tried to explain that artistic ability and entrepreneurial ability are both manifestations of human creativity. Some people have artistic ability and some people don't. The same holds true for entrepreneurship. We can teach entrepreneurs to be better managers and leaders but cannot teach individuals to be entrepreneurs.

MYTH # 15
Becoming An E-business Is Complex And Expensive

In the early 1800's a group of English textile workers, led by Ned Ludd, rebelled over the technological advancements spurred by the industrial revolution. These Luddites, as they were soon known, feared that technology would remove the need for workers, thus they loathed technology and destroyed new machinery whenever possible.

Unfortunately, the Luddite philosophy toward Internet technology is alive and well among many entrepreneurs. It may be human nature to avoid what we don't understand but entrepreneurs who are technophobes are really reducing their likelihood of success. Turning a business into an e-business is not complicated or expensive but it does require a little vision and commitment.

E-business is simply defined as using electronic technology to enhance a company's profitability. The first thing to remember is that building an e-business is similar to building house in that the foundation should be the starting point. The foundation of every e-business is the Business-to-Business (B2B) supply chain. Every business regardless of size or industry can enhance its efficiency within their supply chain by performing functions online.

For instance, Carrier Corporation, a manufacturer of air conditioners, was able to enhance profitability by $100,000,000 per year simply by using the internet to perform human resource management and procurement tasks. Yet, even the smallest businesses can drastically enhance profitability. Imagine a home-based business owner who can reduce her errand time (going to the post office, buying office supplies etc.) by one-hour per week just by performing menial tasks online. This results in 52 hours per year of increased productivity allowing her to spend more time with customers and generating revenue.

Once the B2B infrastructure of a web-site is established entrepreneurs should work with a web-designer to come-up with creative Business-to-Consumer (B2C) features. However, prior to doing that I would encourage them to look at web-sites in an industry other than their own for inspiration. When looking at competitor web-sites it is easy to fall into the trap of simply copying the look and feel of these web-sites. Looking to other industries with regard to e-commerce or any other business process stimulates ideas and innovation.

Consider the story of Henry Ford who was one of three hundred American automobile manufacturers in the early twentieth century. By the time he retired he was one of only three American car manufacturers largely due to the assembly line concept he pioneered. Did you know that Mr. Ford was inspired to develop the assembly line after touring the slaughterhouses of Chicago? Just as an example of what he might have experienced on his tours I have added an excerpt from Upton Sinclair's 1906 book *The Jungle*, which although a work of fiction gave a fairly accurate depiction of the meat packing industry at the time:

The "Union Stockyards" were never a pleasant place; but now they were not only a collection of slaughterhouses, but also the camping place of an army of fifteen or twenty thousand human beasts. All day long the blazing midsummer sun beat down upon that square mile of abominations: upon tens of thousands of cattle crowded into pens whose wooden floors stank and steamed contagion; upon bare, blistering, cinder-strewn railroad tracks, and huge blocks of dingy meat factories, whose labyrinthine passages defied a breath of fresh air to penetrate them; and there were not merely rivers of hot blood, and car-loads of moist flesh, and rendering vats and soap caldrons, glue factories and fertilizer tanks, that smelt like the craters of hell—there were also tons of garbage festering in the sun, and the greasy laundry of the workers hung out to dry, and dining rooms littered with food and black with flies, and toilet rooms that were open sewers.

***

Imagine an entrepreneur who could be inspired by such a sight. Yet, Henry Ford realized that the disassembly lines used by the slaughterhouses could be re-engineered into assembly lines for automobiles, which would reduce costs, reduce prices, and increase demand. Ford Motor Company essentially put 99% of their competitors out of business as a result of borrowing a process from another industry.

There is no reason why entrepreneurs shouldn't follow this line of thinking when developing their web-site. In 2005 I launched *The Entrepreneurship Academy*, an online resource for aspiring entrepreneurs. One of the industries I looked to for inspiration was the media industry. After all, media conglomerates are expert at attracting and retaining viewers. One way they do this is by adding new content daily in the form of streaming video clips. When I went back and looked at my competition I noticed that virtually all of their content was printed. So, I did audio/video presentations that were very well received. If I had followed the lead of my competitors I would have had an informative web-site just not a very fun one.

When it comes time to designing a web-site my suggestion would be to work with an entrepreneur who works full-time in the information technology industry and operates a small side business. These entrepreneurs, from my experience, do not have the financial pressures of full-time entrepreneurs and often charge less for work of equal or superior quality than full-time entrepreneurs. Either way a high-end web-site should not cost more than a couple of thousand dollars. A competent web-designer will walk you through all of the steps needed to securely process payments online.

Research I have seen suggests that internet users generally give a web-site five-to-ten seconds to make a positive impression. If the site looks cheap and/or unprofessional visitors are soon off to the next site. Therefore, you really need to make a strong first impression. A good rule of thumb is to make the web-site easy to navigate by not adding too much text. A picture says a thousand words so if you can express the value proposition of your product or service visually the better off you will be.

MYTH # 16
You Can Become A Self-made Millionaire

There have been a lot of great professional and self-help books written over the years but the absolute greatest of them all, in my opinion, is *Think and Grow Rich* by Napoleon Hill. Written in 1937, it remains a timeless classic as to how to approach life and business opportunities.

The back-story of *Think and Grow Rich* is almost as interesting as the text. Mr. Hill was a young journalist in 1908 when he interviewed Andrew Carnegie for a newspaper assignment. Mr. Carnegie was one of the world's wealthiest men who had risen from dire poverty and was convinced that the secret of success could be taught to average people. Impressed with the young reporter, Mr. Carnegie challenged Mr. Hill to go out and talk to successful people and identify the secret for success.

Mr. Hill took up the challenge and interviewed hundreds of leaders such as John D. Rockefeller, Thomas Edison, and Theodore Roosevelt. Soon patterns began to emerge, which Mr. Hill recorded and published in his book. There were numerous traits that successful people shared including:

Having a Definite Purpose

Of all the things you can do with your time, talent, and money, why did you choose the path you chose? Mr. Hill believed that people that followed their true calling in life were the most successful. Michael Dell, for example, had a definite purpose of becoming the largest computer maker in the world. Today, Dell manufactures more computers than any other company in the world. Such is the power of having a definite purpose as it is the building block for all professional endeavors. One of Mr. Hill's most famous lines from the text is "what your mind can conceive and believe you can achieve." Truer words have never been written.

Positive Mental Attitude

Think of the most negative and cynical person you know. Now think about the most positive person you know. Who is more successful? My guess is that it is the more positive of the two. Not only in professional matters but likely in personal relationships too. People generally don't like to be around cynics but are drawn to optimists. People who can make others feel better shine like a beacon in a sea of negativity and inevitably rise to leadership positions.

It doesn't take any talent to be a cynic but it does take talent, in the form of emotional intelligence, to become a leader. A great quote by Mr. Hill typifies the viewpoint of those possessing a positive mental attitude: "every adversity, every failure, every heartache carries with it the seed of an equal or greater benefit." You have probably heard this quote in many ways, shapes, or forms over the years but successful entrepreneurs truly believe it. Failure is nothing more than the seed of opportunity.

Faith

Mr. Hill placed special emphasis on what he called *Infinite Intelligence*, which essentially means that all of our gifts and talents derive from He who gave us life. In other words, we are a manifestation of God who is infinitely intelligent. If He gave us certain talents then logic would dictate that He intended us to utilize those talents in pursuit of happiness. This was very powerful for me as an 18 year-old entrepreneur when I first read *Think and Grow Rich*. I used to get frustrated by being different but after reading this book I began to believe that being different is not a curse but a blessing. God would not have given me, or you, entrepreneurial talent without providing the opportunity to get the most out of it.

Mr. Hill's book does not espouse a particular religion rather recognizes that you cannot have creation without a Creator. And, He who created Heaven and Earth also created you and me, each with our own gifts and potential. Scientists can debate whether or not the universe is nothing but a cosmic accident and that we are nothing more than the byproducts of some primordial soup. The important thing about Mr. Hill's research is that his interview subjects believed that they were endowed with special gifts and had an obligation to get the most out of them.

Faith is nothing more than belief in the absence of proof. If you have faith in God then you should have faith in yourself too, since you are an expression of His infinite intelligence.

Master Mind Alliances

In his famous book *Free to Choose* economist Milton Friedman asks the question "how many people does it take to make a pencil?" The answer is that it takes thousands of people to make even the simplest product. Consider the labor it takes to process the wood, build machinery, make the trucks that haul the wood etc. Every variable is impacted by numerous other variables and no one variable is more important than the others. The employee who chops down a tree is just as important as the employee who places the finished pencil in its box.

Entrepreneurship is very similar. In America we love the notion of being a self-made millionaire but millionaires will be the first ones to tell you that they didn't do it alone. It takes the help of family members, employees, mentors, teachers, customers, and vendors. Napoleon Hill referred to this personal and professional network as a Master Mind Alliance.

So, who should comprise your master mind alliance? The answer is found by looking inward and carefully analyzing your limitations. Pride is perhaps the greatest entrepreneurial sin. Entrepreneurs who ignore their weaknesses or think they have none generally fall victim to them. The best strategy is to understand your weaknesses then develop a group of stakeholders (employees, vendors, strategic partners etc.) whose strengths compensate for those weaknesses. This allows the entrepreneur to focus primarily on his/her strengths and passion.

For example, researchers long ago recognized that the personalities and skill sets of individuals are often dictated by what side of their brain is more dominant. Left-brain people tend to be more logical and analytical (engineers, accountants etc.) and right-brain people tend to be more creative and verbal (artists, sales professionals etc.). In an established corporation there is an eclectic set of individuals whose strengths compensate for each others weaknesses. The right-brained organizationally challenged sales rep gives a purchase order to the left-brained impersonal accountant and all is well. Executives know that the weaknesses of the sales reps are mitigated by the strengths of the accountants.

In a start-up the entrepreneur simultaneously serves as sales rep and accountant and the likelihood is that he/she is stronger in one area than the other. Therefore, rather than spending time working on overcoming weaknesses savvy entrepreneurs find alliances to perform tasks outside their expertise. It may be in the form of strategic partnerships, outsourcing, hiring professional service providers or recruiting employees. The simple premise is: focus on your strengths and find people to compensate for your weaknesses.

MYTH #17
If It's Not Broken…Don't Fix It

One of the most dangerous times of an entrepreneur's career is the point where he/she becomes content. Contentment is a sort of entrepreneurial paradox in that we should all strive to be content but once we achieve it the prognosis for future entrepreneurial success is limited.

In a corporate or government setting it is possible for people to simply go through the motions, perform the same tasks year-after-year, and essentially hang on to their jobs until retirement. Unfortunately, the content entrepreneur's business has the life expectancy of a content Zebra on the African plains. It might survive in the short term but eventually less content Lions will pounce.

Just to prove a point try placing a $1 bill in this book and come back in a year and take it out. The future value of that $1 bill will be about ninety-six cents. Similarly, businesses are assets that lose value if you do not have them work for you. As an entrepreneur you are essentially either moving forward or you're moving backward. If it seems like you are standing still you are really moving backward without even knowing it. You may still have an asset but like that $1 bill your business will be worth less than it could be if you are not proactive.

True, you say, but what if the business owner is nearing retirement or is simply tired and doesn't want to grow the business anymore? My advice would be for him/her to either sell the business or begin thinking like a mentor. A great way to grow a business is to bring in new people who have vision and talent. The entrepreneur may find leadership and mentorship very rewarding. Growing a business is very hard, and it's even harder when an entrepreneur and his/her employees are experiencing professional stagnation. Bringing in new employees shakes things up and jumpstarts creativity. Of course, long time employees may resent this and the culture may resist it. However, research clearly demonstrates that the corporate culture of a business where the founding entrepreneur is actively involved in operations reflects that entrepreneur's personality. Essentially, if the founder remains entrepreneurial so will the culture.

A sure way to determine if an entrepreneur is falling into the cage of contentment is to review the five functions of management: planning, organizing, staffing, leading and controlling.

Planning—This is the most important of management as it sets the tone for all future decision making. Every company should have a 2-3 year business plan, which is comprised of separate human resource; marketing; and finance plans. These plans set qualitative goals and quantitative objectives for the company. If the company doesn't have a written plan the entrepreneur may be content.

Organizing—Allocating tangible and intangible assets is one of the more challenging aspects of entrepreneurship. When Apple Computer has a product flop, as it did in the early 1980's with its Lisa Computer, their losses can be written-off and the company moves along to the their next venture. When small businesses have a flop it's not as easy to recover and entrepreneurs know this intuitively. Therefore, they often hesitate to allocate resources to new projects, which results in creative stagnation and inevitably a loss of market share. A way of overcoming this threat is to allocate a percentage of revenue for Research and Development (R&D).

Staffing—A sure way to tell when an entrepreneur is becoming content is when they begin to think that their brand is their greatest asset. Brands are important but they are really nothing more than consumer perceptions influenced by employee actions. A great brand is nothing, therefore, but the fruit of the organizational tree. Great brands are built by great people. Hence employees are a firm's greatest asset. Employers who are content to plug anyone into a position assuming they will maintain product quality are sadly mistaken. Building a superior brand requires superior employee recruitment, training, and leadership.

Leadership—Various definitions of leadership can be found in the academic literature and many include the concept of having a network of loyal followers. I take issue with these definitions because I think someone can have loyal followers without really leading anyone anywhere. The two questions I ask entrepreneurs to identify if they are truly leading are: do your competitors respect your ability to continuously add value for your stakeholders and; are your stakeholders more advanced (personally and professionally) today than they were yesterday? If you answer yes to both those questions you are an entrepreneurial leader. If you answer no you are probably content.

Controlling—This facet of management simply involves making sure that pre-set quality standards are being met and the objectives outlined in the business plan are being met. Essentially, controlling is simply making sure you are actually doing what you said you were going to do. Ways to set realistic expectations include benchmarking the company's performance against competitor and industry standards and conducting trend analysis. If the company is failing to meet goals and objectives the likelihood is that a culture of contentment is present within the organization.

MYTH #18
Viable Ideas Are Hard To Identify

Over the years I have worked with hundreds of aspiring entrepreneurs and most of them have a good vision of what they want to accomplish. However, sometimes people have a burning desire to start a business but they just don't know where to begin. Essentially, they cannot find an opportunity to pursue. One place to begin is by asking "what's next?" Every product has a life cycle and every industry faces competitive pressures. Therefore, it is essential that you ask "what's next? What product or service could replace the need for an existing product or service?" The entrepreneur who correctly answers the question "what's next?" will reap the financial rewards. Entrepreneurs that don't ask what's next are in big trouble.

For example, in 1997 entrepreneur Philippe Kahn invented the camera phone. By the year 2000 Sharp and Vodafone were partnering to sell camera phones to awaiting consumers throughout the world. In 2001, Polaroid Corporation, whose founder invented the concept of instant photography over 50 years earlier, filed for bankruptcy. How do executives at a company like Polaroid, who had a half-century head start, overlook an opportunity like camera phones? They forgot to ask "what's next". What will the next cell phone advancement bring? Who knows, but rest assured in the years to come there will be integration between the functions of a credit card and your cell phone. Just hand your cell phone to a cashier, wait as he/she scans the bar code, and see your grocery charges appear on your cell phone bill.

In 1960, Theodore Levitt wrote an article called *Marketing Myopia* for Harvard Business Review, which discussed how the Railroad companies had a stranglehold on the nation's transportation infrastructure in the late 1800's. They thought they were invincible, which ultimately led to their marginalization. Rail transportation is still with us, but how often do you ride the train? Not often I'd bet. Professor Levitt went on to explain in the article that the fundamental mistake made by railroad company executives at the time was thinking they were in the railroad business rather than the transportation business. If they had correctly viewed themselves as transportation executives they might have invested in fledgling concepts such as the automobile and airplane.

Regardless of their industry entrepreneurs need to continuously identify what's next. Here is one tip of finding it: ask your master-mind alliance as they may have the answer. The next thing does not have to revolutionary, just evolutionary. Former McDonald's CEO Ray Kroc was famous for soliciting feedback from franchisees whose opinion he valued due to their proximity to customers. The Filet-O-Fish concept was conceived by a Cincinnati franchisee whose Catholic customers did not want to eat meat on Fridays. The concept of the Egg McMuffin, which led to McDonald's foray into the breakfast business, was conceived by a California franchisee who simply contacted Mr. Kroc with an idea for a new sandwich.

If you believe that within every problem lay the seed of opportunity finding what's next may be as simple as looking for problems in your workplace and identifying solutions. It doesn't have to be complicated it just has to solve a problem.

One of my more lucrative ventures was in the area of food safety consulting. During my manufacturing venture I became certified by the U.S. Food and Drug Administration to implement Hazard Analysis at Critical Control Point (HACCP) plans. HACCP is a process whereby you identify and mitigate physical, biological, and chemical hazards within a foodservice and/or manufacturing setting. Within a week of attaining my certification (which cost about $300) I was developing HACCP plans (charging $125 per hour) for manufacturers who needed to comply with new FDA requirements.

I simply looked at an industry that I knew intimately and asked: what's next? In this case it was the need to increase food safety standards. A little trend analysis identified that the average food borne illness lawsuit cost restaurant owners $75,000. For just a few hundred dollars a month I could greatly reduce their risk. They had a problem, I had a solution. Sometimes it is really that simple. From this point forward you should get excited anytime you hear about a business problem as this is the first step toward identifying a profitable solution.

MYTH # 19
The Government Is Not Your Friend

I think I'm on fairly safe ground when I say that nobody likes to pay taxes. However, if you begin looking at the government as a stakeholder and taxes as an investment you'll find that you can generate a good return-on-investment.

A few years ago I received a call from a food broker friend who asked me if there were any opportunities for American seafood processors in Italy. It turns out that a client of his who had developed a process for cooking and quick freezing whole Maine Lobsters was approached by an executive of an Italian resort about the possibility of shipping the lobster to Italy. My friend was interested in knowing if there were more opportunities like this throughout the country.

Living in Rhode Island at the time I thought to myself "how do I know?" I'm fortunate to be well educated but the dining habits of your average Italian are a bit outside of my realm of knowledge. But I said "let me find out." Within an hour I had developed a one page management brief identifying that the United States consulate in Italy had recently identified the sale of frozen seafood, including lobster, as an opportunity for American companies. To glean this information I simply went to the USDA's website and did a search for Lobster and Italy. Dozens of valid research articles from various government agencies came back discussing domestic and international opportunities as well as helpful trend analysis.

Federal and state agencies perform this type of research on virtually every industry and it is a treasure trove of information. Often the information high-priced consultants provide for clients is gleaned from free governmental sources. The 40-point sanitation checklist I developed for my food safety clients was based on free templates provided by the Food and Drug Administration. IRS and OSHA consultants are doing the same thing. Why re-invent the wheel? If the government is going to do the work for you let them. It is in the best interest of the government, the entrepreneur, and the client.

Entrepreneurs in all industries should also look to the government (state, local and federal) as potential customers. Did you know that the U.S. government is the largest consumer in the world? Get on the Federal Register web-site and take a look at what the government buys. It is amazing. Yes, they buy a lot of rockets and bombs. However, they also buy landscaping services, hire consultants, order oil changes for government vehicles etc. You name it and the government likely buys it.

Registering as a U.S. government approved vendor is easy. Your starting point should be www.business.gov. You should also check out the Small Business Administration web-site since many large government contractors must by law outsource a percentage of their work on government contracts to small businesses and particularly women and minority owned businesses.

It is easy to look at the government as threat, after all the ROI of the money you give them in taxes isn't always immediately recognizable. But you have to pay, one way or the other. Those entrepreneurs who cheat on their taxes are lowering their taxes but are simultaneously lowering the value of their business. If you don't declare income you are minimizing your sales data, which is the basis for the discounted cash-flow method of business valuation. When it comes time to sell the business those cheating entrepreneurs have shot themselves in the foot because, on paper, the business is not profitable. Who wants to buy an unprofitable business?

The area where the government is perhaps your greatest ally is in the area of intellectual property. If you have an idea for an invention or for a new use for an existing product the United States Patent and Trademark Office should be your first stop. They will walk you through the process of documenting your idea; developing a provisional patent (patent pending status); and attaining a patent. There are various types of patents but the USPTO does a nice job of walking you through the requirements. If you are granted a patent you have the sole right to sell the product for 20 years. As you can imagine, if your product has real market viability a fortune can be made.

Not to be overlooked is the government's role in protecting our brand identity. On the day you conceive the idea for a logo, image, or company name you should do a trademark search on www.uspto.gov. If there are no hits that means you have not infringed on any registered trademarks, which are denoted with ®. Entrepreneurs do not however, need to register a trademark to be afforded protection. They just need to place a TM next to their intellectual property. If there is a dispute between companies the company that can demonstrate using the trademark in commerce first will win. Conflicts arise more than you might think. Come up with a creative name for a web-site, for example, and do a search for its availability. You may find someone claimed the name and holds the rights to it even if they are not commercially using it.

MYTH # 20
Goliath Is Unbeatable

One of the things that strikes fear into the heart of even the savviest entrepreneur is the prospect of Wal-Mart, or another huge competitor, moving into their marketing area. However, not only is this scenario an opportunity for small businesses it will likely be the best thing that ever happened to them if they adopt a customer centric approach.

To prove this point it would be easy to find a small business that has carved a profitable niche, but I don't want you to feel as if you will need to be relegated to niche status. After all, every big business was once a small business. I firmly believe that the reason many businesses stay small is because their leaders do not think big.

Let's look at a once small entrepreneurial venture called *Sound of Music*, which opened for business in 1966. *Sound of Music* is today *Best Buy*, which has been successful in a very competitive market by adopting strategies that all entrepreneurs should emulate including being focused on customer needs, maximizing supply chain efficiency, and empowering employees. A good way to go from being a small business to a big business is to replicate proven formulas. While entrepreneurship is an art, marketing and management are sciences. Apply the following business processes that *Best Buy* is using to your venture and watch how fast the business grows.

Let's start with an overview of the company. *Best Buy* is a specialty retailer of consumer electronics, computer software, home appliances, and home office products. With more than 830 stores the company ranks among the top 100 growth firms by Fortune magazine. The Minneapolis-based company has diversified through an aggressive acquisition strategy, e-commerce, and is experiencing exponential growth in the professional services sector via their Geek Squad business unit.

In 1980 Harvard Professor Michael Porter put forth the five forces model of competitive analysis, which companies can use to gauge their competitive landscape. While I am applying a five forces analysis for *Best Buy* I would like you to think about how you can use this type of analysis to position your company to compete with larger competitors. Again, every big company was once a small company. If you are going to grow your venture into an industry leader you need to think strategically.

Best Buy operates in what would best be described as an oligopoly environment (an industry controlled by several major players) with their primary competitors being Wal-Mart and Circuit City. Additionally, Best Buy's online division completes directly with formidable competitors such as Dell and Amazon.com. Using the Porter's five forces model it is evident that *Best Buy* is positioned well for continued growth but also faces significant competitive threats.

Intensity of rivalry among competitors

The competition among large electronics retailers is fierce and something that plays an important role in *Best Buy's* executive level decision making. For example, at *Best Buy's* corporate headquarters employees entering the building see a mock triage unit replete with bandages and litters. This is an unsubtle metaphorical reminder to employees of what will happen to the company if they take their eye off Wal-Mart.

Wal-Mart executives, of course, are also intensely focused on *Best Buy*. This is evident by the fact that Wal-Mart has been modifying a number of its electronics departments in an effort to create a more customer centric retail environment. *Best Buy's* focus is on customer centricity, which is essentially de-centralizing control and empowering store-level managers and employees to tailor offerings and displays that reflect the needs of local customers. According to *Best Buy's* 2006 annual report this strategy has contributed to a 22% increase in same store sales in fiscal 2006 and is the cornerstone of the *Best Buy* corporate strategy moving forward.

The previous paragraph tells us the importance of focusing on the relationship with your customer rather than fixating on pricing. Wal-Mart is going to win every pricing battle but the area where smaller companies can beat them is in customer service. *Best Buy* has recognized this and so too must entrepreneurs who hope to compete against larger competitors.

Pressure from substitute products

Best Buy executives recognize that high-volume retailers like Wal-Mart, and online retailers, like Dell, potentially have the ability to undercut their costs, which will corresponding reduce their market share. Thus, they have developed a series of partnerships with electronics manufacturers in China to produce their own products under various brand names, which reduces the risk of losing market-share to lower cost substitute products. While vertical integration mitigates the risk of substitute products, *Best Buy* has further mitigated the risk by offering value-added services such as extended warranties and technical services.

While entrepreneurs should also continuously be seeking to reduce costs by outsourcing (where appropriate) and achieving supply chain efficiencies, the best way to mitigate the risk of substitute products is by delving into services. It is harder to replicate a service so entrepreneurs need to think about what service they can provide that others cannot. For example, have you ever notice how doctors and lawyers (both among the highest paid professions) tend to specialize in certain areas? If you have a recurring headache are you going to see a neurologist or a family practitioner? If you can tailor your expertise to a service, rather than a product, you will be better positioned in the long run.

Barriers to entry

One of the major advantages of operating as part of an oligopoly is that there are, from the perspective of the big company executives, few competitors. For example, big-box retailers like Wal-Mart know the huge capital costs associated with building a retail infrastructure reduces the likelihood of new entrants. The cost of capital associated with retail along with ancillary human resource and marketing expenses result in a significant barrier to entry for up-start competitors. However, smaller retailers can take advantage if the fact that the big companies do not view them as competition by exploiting their weaknesses. Whole Foods, an organic grocery retailer, illustrates this principle perfectly. Noting that the large supermarket chains were selling only mass produced products and were treating their customers poorly, Whole Foods began distributing organic foods and creating a retail environment that promoted a community feeling.

I can tell you from having spent much of my early career in the grocery industry that the established retail chains never took these "tree huggers" seriously and it cost them dearly. Today, based on the success and superior profit margin percentages of companies like Whole Foods you see the big retailers trying to emulate the natural foods stores by offering healthier organic fare. However, they never seem to capture the spirit and ambiance of the natural food stores.

Bargaining power of buyers (customers)

Best Buy management appears to be acutely aware of the number of options consumers have. In an effort to mitigate the power of buyers the company has been aggressive in promoting extended warranties, which serve the purpose of maintaining a relationship with buyers and increasing their switching costs. While *Best Buy's* aggressive approach to selling warranties has drawn the ire of some consumer groups it continues to be a significant source of revenue.

This is an area that entrepreneurs will also want to focus intently. Many small business owners fail to measure the projected lifetime value of their customers. It is easier to retain an existing customer than it is to attract a new one. Therefore, every entrepreneur should institute some sort of customer relationship management program that will increase the buyers switching cost (making it less convenient and costly to switch to another company). Warranties may be one way to do this but not the only way. Loyalty programs are something every entrepreneur should institute because they are low cost and give the customer a true sense that you value their patronage. While many large companies have affinity programs, which provide discounts based on certain purchases, loyalty programs should seek to provide real quantitative and qualitative value. Qualitative value would include incorporating customer feedback back into the research and development process.

Bargaining power of suppliers

One of the keys to *Best Buy's* growth has been the effective management of its supply chain and communication with its vendors. The company has established a comprehensive vendor extranet where terms of vendor expectations are clearly articulated.

Relationships between large retailers and their supply chain partners have changed considerably over the past decade, largely due to the success achieved by Wal-Mart. This balance of power, from manufacturer to retailer, mitigates the supplier risks *Best Buy* faces considerably. Also, this risk is further reduced by the firm's vertical integration strategy. Of course, manufacturers with products that are in high demand will have more power than those who don't, but the relationship between *Best Buy* and its vendor base appears to by relatively symbiotic. As the largest consumer electronics retailer in the world, *Best Buy* appears to have more leverage than their vendors but don't appear to be wielding it unethically.

The realtionship a small business has with its vendors is also essential and even the smallest business should seek to get its supply chain integrated elecronically. Towards this end an extranet can be established that links the company's internal processes (purchasing, logistics, professional services etc.). Integrating an extranet, as well as an intranet that facilitates communication among a company's employess can be integrated into your company's web site for a modest fee by most web-designers.

By examining the growth of *Best Buy* from a small start-up to industry leader we can see the benefits of thinking big but also the benefits of thinking small (maintaing close relationships with customers). Essentially, the key to their success has been effectively managing their supply chain, staying focused on growth, and maintaining a customer centric culture. These are three things that you will also need to do if your business is to become the an industry leader.

www.ingramcontent.com/pod-product-compliance
Lightning Source LLC
Chambersburg PA
CBHW071238170526
45165CB00003B/1155